tom weber

halfway to blossoming

scribbles of a mind in slumber

Bibliographische Information der Deutschen Nationalbibliothek:

Die Deutsche Nationalbibliothek verzeichnet diese Publikation in der Deutschen Nationalbibliographie; detaillierte bibliographische Daten sind im Internet über http://dnb.dnb.de abrufbar.

Herstellung und Verlag:
BoD - Books on Demand, Norderstedt

ISBN: 978-3-7504-3420-2

<u>bardo</u>

In Tibetan Buddhism a period of transition. The most well-known bardos are

kyenay bardo (the bardo of birth and this life)

milam bardo (the bardo of dreams)

samten bardo (the bardo of meditation)

chikhai bardo (the bardo of the moment of death)

chönyi bardo (the bardo of the luminosity of the true nature)

sidpa bardo (the bardo of becoming or transmigration)

However, generally speaking any period of transition is regarded as a "bardo"

<u>māra</u>

Buddhist demon described by Nyanaponika Thera as "the personification of the forces antagonistic to enlightenment".

Māra makes use of five emotions (called "arrows") to persuade practitioners to give up meditation.

- the arrow that makes one ecstatic

- the arrow that makes one crave

- the arrow that makes one stupefied (spaced out)

- the arrow that makes one worn out, hungry or thirsty

- the arrow that makes one afraid of dying

For A.

*the most beautiful coincidence I could
have ever encountered*

kyenay bardo

recognising the waves

sip

colourful streams
rain down on me

blue and yellow
and green and red
and orange and pink

big fat drops of life
juicy thick and sweet

i like watching them
slowly rolling down
a reflecting skin

trying to work out
how to get in

i like to think
about the colours

and what they could mean
and what they could bring

if they'd finally find
a way in

out of place

the man in the white room
sits patiently

and observes

the blankness around him
it shapes

the curve of his sight

there are no colours
in the white room
just words

sometimes
they lie
defeated

in a supposed corner

sometimes
they come too close
but those are at least true

in her left
she balances

the knife

its warm blade
always mirrors

a happy face

she is never sad
when she looks into the blade

in his right
he holds on to

the glass

even he doesn't
know anymore

what's in it

but it always
mirrors

a sad face

he is never happy
when he looks into the glass

the woman in the black room
doesn't exist

i wrote her
but then again

she wrote me

a writer's birthday card

happy birthday to you
a grey man whispers
through curtains of flesh

happy birthday to you
spectre asking himself
where is this man

happy birthday to you
who goes by so many
chosen names

happy birthday to you
wind that keeps blowing
what can never move

happy birthday to you
man of many shadows
who yearns for a drop of light

sincerely and with all my love
gloomy winter days for us
and a happy birthday to you!

A.

hey there little bird
come sit on my hand

still trembling

it has just written
another poem
carved the silent
but still hopeful
questions in
the whiteness of
this paper

as blank as this present

is right now

but do sit
the shaking

usually

stops for a moment

oh look at you
you're made out of glass!
how wonderful

how boring

i still see
the same things
in this

prison of freedom

maybe i should melt you?
yes that i'll do

as i feel the scalding
hot glass
running down

my stiff fingers

i can see new again
in what was always there

and i remember

i am where i am
because of them
i am who i am
because of you
i become who i become
because of us

try harder

years ago
i wandered off

the bleak path
paved for us
couldn't hold me

any longer

i entered
a forest
darker than
every night

and searched
for the light

from the inside
of a dead tree
a single spark

was gifted to me

a whisper
now lost
in time

and the emptiness
of the main road
slowly faded away

but so did you

"don't worry"
i told you
"please
carry on
i'll be fine"

i was always good at that

i grabbed my chest
held it firmly
and opened it up

the warmth of this spark
now next to
a longing heart

and so i carried on
through the forest
scared but still there

until i found
another spark

"i'm sorry
i have one
right here"
i said pointing
at my chest

but in this
darkness
who am i
to just leave

a spark

i need to do more

always good
to have a knife

i balance it
in my right hand
before i start
opening up again

i carve away
at the useless flesh
until the hole
seems big enough
for two

"come inside"
i say with
a trembling voice

two sparks
they take up
so much
too much

space

my heart
starts getting
in the way

weakened
i go on
through a
place i don't
see anymore

oh no

another spark

boo

"my reflection
seems nice"

says the poet

and shoots himself

know-it-alls

protests all around the globe

ugh

why can't young people be grateful
for the world that we have built?

it could be so much worse
i mean

it's not like we live in a world
where people are exploited
for the profit of a few

it's not like we live in a world
where we discriminate against
people because of

their gender
their skin colour
their religion
their sexual orientation

i mean those young people
should be grateful

that we don't pay
women less than men
for the same work

that we don't equate
refugees to terrorists

that we don't ask
people of colour
to distance themselves

if one of them does something wrong
while never asking the same

of white people

these young people are so ungrateful
i mean it's not like we live in world

where we let some 100 companies
destroy our planet

just to make even more money

it's not like we live in a world
where we complained for years

that young people have no interest
in politics

but then also complain when they
do rise up

because we don't like
what they have to say

yeah if we lived in a world like that

then they should speak up
but could you even imagine

if our world was that fucked up

never back down

i lie

deep down in
reeking grounds

the soil
and dust
from above

is slowly
drying out

my skin

the once so
carefully crafted

paring

over me
i see

them cheerfully
throwing down

blocks
of
gold

and other

delusions of

the good man

burying me
under a pile

of promises
never really meant

they have to work harder

every day

the graves are getting

deeper

while they are getting

fewer

my fallen sisters
my fallen brothers
they bleed with me

in unison

to soak this
ransacked earth

in a red

so warm and bright

the masters up above
they don't know it yet

our blood makes the
flowers grow

among which one day
our children will

once again

change the world
and rip open

the graves
where we lie

ignored but not forgotten

to william blake

in metropolitan streets i saw a man
under a statue of great marianne.
he was on the ground just lying there
his face shimmering from sweat like a flare.

his hair and beard wild and untamed
the flees his only friends that remained.
around his cracked lips there was a frame
of vomit his lifestyle subtly to disclaim.

down his nose ran like a peaceful stream
some snot dull yellow with a hint of green.
it all sparkled wonderfully in the light of day
and reflected our people ready to array.

on his shirt there was a peculiar design
a blotch of alcohol maybe some wine.
of course the slim red stripes could come
from the knife resting besides his thumb.

many people saw this unobtrusive shape
most walked right by trying to escape.
i myself looked at this fractured gem
before shrugging and joining them.

over aleppo skies

over aleppo skies
a bomb fell
into children's hearts

a subtitle in the paper
proclaimed it
less lofty:

"battle for aleppo: civilian casualties mount"

target: a school
of course
the evil hoard
where it is taught
to think for yourself

i cannot wait
for the explanation
they come up with
this time

the wind?
technical problems?

how about

crimes against humanity
that one would be new

and don't you worry mr. president

america was first

when over aleppo skies
a bomb fell
into children's hearts

the wasteland

come down to the wasteland
and witness what we've done

debris has crushed the people
fires have burned their homes

water is no more just tears
tears from smoke and tears from loss

holy walls were blown to smithereens
by bombs sold for someone's profit

"this is defence" they tell us
dead babies sure pose no more threat

but come down to the wasteland
and witness one more thing

a little girl among the dead
is walking on what seems to have been a street

see her dress in all those colours
which still shine through our dust

and the flower she has stitched
onto her scarred pulsing chest

she lifts a brick off
a dead man's face

takes the flower off herself
and puts it in his broken mouth

come down to the wasteland
and hear our victims sing

srebrenica

not far
from his house

the flowers have

long since

returned

the trees have

not forgotten
not forgiven

sentenced
to guard

over

the shreds of humanity
which

they spit

in a burrow
like

used gum

not far

from his house

they lie hastily buried
under the flowers

which already sprout again

this poem was originally written in Serbian and then
translated into English

gaps

thwarted crescendo
in a boiling night
consume the silence
and the blankness of
a word not written

acknowledgment

to love
at first sight

and be intrigued

to love
at the first glances

and be curious

to love
at the first conversation shared

and feel a warmth around my heart

to love
the first poem you sent me

and be fascinated

to love
the way you laugh

and can't help but smile

to love
the way you care about this world

and feel inspired

to love
your faults

and feel empathy towards you

to love
your mind

and have great respect for you

to love
your pragmatism

and know i might have floated away without it

to love
your gentleness

and fall for you each day anew

to love
your strength

and always be on your side

to love
that you want what is best

and trust you forever and always

to love
your sense of beauty

and keep on writing for you

to love you
is an honour

a pleasure
and a pride

to love you
makes me want to be better

loving you
has made me realise

muses give their authors
books to write
and hymns to sing

but only you
could give me peace

bi5anz IO

grandeur

symphony of
an unfocused

surreal understanding

pictures captured
between pressed

fibre

a silence
so deafening

your fingers
get stuck

on the turning point

of a once
beautifully rhymed

existence

soliloquy

i've known
the invisible man

for quite some time

now

she was always there
kind of

but only really came

into existence
when i

gave him a name

at first

he only watched
carefully

expectantly

then she started
talking
getting

LOUDER

every day

but i managed
to ignore

him

for a long time

then however
came

yes

i still do

i remember the day

the invisible man cut
off his

tongue

and shoved it down my throat

deep down inside
of me
it still

lies

today

her words are
impossible to ignore

today

they haunt me
they keep me awake

on nights like these
and

leave me with no

choice

except to listen
while

the invisible woman

watches curiously
with a bleeding smile

holiday on anthemoessa

i ask of you don't hold it against me
but i love to hear the sirens sing
i like to get lost i like to be free
of the burden of my own will
just from time to time

just from time to time

i dwell in a magical land
where all egos merge
where past present and future
combine into a symphony
and all existence beautifully rhymes

and all existence beautifully rhymes

in the shivering depths of
this kaleidoscope left behind
where the light in our eyes
gets set free upon touching
the prism of our minds

mountain song

for years i have described

the lonely man

walking on a path
unknown to him

living a life
u n s u r e to him

and i always wondered
what keeps him going

why are his steps so secure
on this scarred ground

i always wondered

about the lonely man

until
i heard

coming far from

the mountains

in the distant past
in the distant future

a song
woven a long time ago

played on a single stem

of a gorgeous
exotic

flower

and i understood

the lonely man

you're not lonely at all

are you

those mountains
that keep her safe

they will always be your destination

and her song
your
our

will always bring

those tears of joy
of true happiness

to those eyes
that still remember

the first time they saw

the most beautiful flower
up

in the mountains

the poet's calling

just some words drifting
what could they bring
the air it is too thick
nowadays

just some words drifting
whom could they help
ears are sealed off
nowadays

just some words drifting
what could they change
when change is poison from the left
nowadays...

nowadays
maybe this is all you need
to reach a heart
to give some love
to consider someone else
to feel for those
who have felt too much

just some words drifting

towards a warm blue sky

ט

needle rotating
on a brown
        k
          e
            n

chest

needle spinning
on what's left

will you be able
to emerge

the final notes of red

still for you but it's me now

cigarette smoke
of a long gone
winter

looms in broken

a

    i

  r

blown away

by an endlessly
moist breath

of never ending spring

before awakening

buried

behind meaty brown
curtains

lies dormant
the bluest

of all flowers

ready to blossom
among the

mysterious red lips
of the eternal infant

samten bardo

hugging māra

being

oh blossom of those
winters past

since we found each other
on that lonesome day

i only ever wanted
to hold on

to your beauty
to your tender
fragile soul

so i held you
in my fist

clenching my fingers
nearly breaking
their dark brown bones

i was so afraid
that you would fall

that i would lose
the purest thing

inside my soul

but just when
you were almost
soaked by the blood

dripping from those
desperate fingers

i finally saw
what made you shine

and so i turn
my broken hand

i cease my grasp
and let you rest

on my open palm

i will never lose you now
as you slowly fade away

into the foggy nights
of those winters past

dawn

for years
a demon's

heavy weight

dragged me down
towards cold barren ground
but

just yesterday

i started rocking him
like a little brother

and we both laughed
as we journeyed

together

towards a warm green field

cypher

a nib
a perfume bottle

both made out of glass

two but one
one but two

separate yet together

the colours seem brighter
than four years ago

weather

clouds passing through
never noticed

the air between them

raindrops pouring down
never noticed

the gaps between them

thunderbolts crashing down
never noticed

the space between them

sunshine after the storm
never noticed

the time between them

storm after sunshine
never noticed

myself between them

coincidence

out of endless possibilities
there emerged a mess
of labels that thought

i

and that bundle of
anxiety
some time later
also thought

you

this concept
is in love

with an illusion

but somehow
knowing how much
of a coincidence

you & i

really were

it makes this
smiling ball of stress

love his illusion

more than ever before

mirage

synapses chatting
synapses thinking
synapses raging
synapses crying
synapses plotting
synapses laughing
synapses scolding
synapses panicking
synapses screaming
synapses gossiping
synapses discussing
synapses hating
synapses wanting
synapses masturbating
synapses creating
synapses ignoring
synapses loving

eyes opening

breath

moonlight streams
across an outer
shell

the songs of the past
not yet forgotten

the silk strings
of the conceptual mind

glitter in the reflected glint
of a pristine forest lake

drop

beams of light
shooting between

compounded ideas

in a single moment
with the conditions
just right

he dared to let
it all go
and with no effort at all

the glass wall shattered
while remaining stable

recognition
a smile

and

hug

hello māra
my old friend

how long has it been?
wow really? i have to say
you have aged like

a fine wine

but seriously we know
each other since...wow
unbelievable

we have been

inseparable

over all those years
haven't we?

you were always there
always
and i listened to you
always

what? i should stop?
but māra, dear, why
would you want me to stop?

kill you? ahahahaha
oh māra your dark sense
of humour still amuses me!

oh wait

you really think so?
māra! why would i
do such a thing?

we had a wonderful time
even when it often didn't
seem like that

it is now time to rest
not just for me
but for both of us
come here māra

you deserve peace too

breeze

glowing notes
bouncing on

an aquarelle landscape

as the fox rests
underneath an ancient tree

you can hear
the earth moving
in a distant field

as the seed slowly grows

vow

and so with a
smile of contentment

the endless sky is
reflected in tears

as the eyes
acknowledge the sun

but the hand
filled with compassion

touches the earth

warmth

as the grain of sand
was about to leave

it realised that

the sun

shines on everything

it settled down
content with itself
and became

the emperor of the universe

tip

as you go on
just think

about those posters
commonly seen

in train stations
and remember

Mind The Gap

contents

tom weber was born in 1996
in luxembourg

since 2014, he writes and
publishes literary texts

photo by philippe bourhis

final whispers

it's every day that has ever been and ever will be.
only you are talking.

mr w: it's weird seeing you like this.

mr v:

mr w: we spent so much time together. at one
point i actually thought you were our only hope.

mr v:

mr w: even after all that has happened i still
loved you. i really did.

mr v:

mr w: you were my most powerful creation. i felt
terribly weak at times because you were so
convincing. in fact i couldn't even see that you are
just an illusion.

mr v:

mr w: there was never a division. it's all a
creation isn't it? not just you, all of it is.

mr v:

mr w: even i am. even *he* is.

mr v:

mr w: thank you old friend. sincerely. without you
pushing me to my limits i could never have
realised this.

mr v:

mr w: i should leave this bench now. this journey
has only just begun.

you leave the bench. all that is left is a beautiful hibiscus
flower, halfway to blossoming.

¡Ultreya! We'll be fine!
Two friends on their Camino to Santiago

"Is this going to work out?" No other question was asked as often as this one when it came to the project "Tom & Jo's Camino for Charity 2019". And you could see why: a Buddhist writer and a Catholic hedonist going on a pilgrimage? Through this book you can relive this peculiar journey from Porto to Santiago de Compostela along the Portuguese Coastal Way in an authentic and engaging manner. See the adventure through Tom's original journal notes, countless pictures and Jo's favourite parts of each day.

A charming testimony of what pilgrimage can mean to a generation born into a materialistic and turbo-capitalist society.

Available as a premium hardcover edition
and as an affordable ebook